Series 536

CONTENTS

BRITISH WILD ANIMALS

by GEORGE CANSDALE
illustrated by
ROLAND GREEN, M.B.O.U., F.R.S.A.

Publishers: Ladybird Books Ltd . Loughborough
© Ladybird Books Ltd (formerly Wills & Hepworth Ltd) 1958
Printed in England

Common Shrew and Mole

The Mole and the Common Shrew belong to the same animal family, but they are not a bit alike in appearance.

The Mole's eyes are tiny and its sight is not good, but this does not matter, because it spends all its life burrowing, finding worms by using its sensitive nose. The fur coat of the Mole is like velvet, and so it can move backwards or forwards in its tunnel without rubbing the fur the wrong way.

. . . .

The Common Shrew is one of the least of the furry animals, and three of them together only weigh an ounce. It is always hungry, and life is one long round of eating worms, grubs, and insects of all kinds, when it is not sleeping.

Shrews have a very strong smell and although some animals kill them, not many are actually eaten.

4

7214 0095 7

Hedgehog

The Hedgehog cannot possibly be mistaken for any other animal, because from the day it is born it is covered with spines. At first these are soft, but by the time the little Hedgehog is only three weeks old, the spines are stiff and sharp.

Hedgehogs are very useful creatures, and it is a good thing to have living in a garden. They eat slugs, caterpillars, beetles, and other pests. Hedgehogs soon become quite tame, but it is best not to keep them as ordinary pets.

If a Hedgehog is living in your garden you can put out a saucer of milk each night, in the same place, for a treat. However, let the Hedgehog find most of its own food and choose its own sleeping place, as well as a cosy corner where it can sleep for most of the winter.

Noctule and
Long-eared Bat

There are more than twelve different kinds of Bats which live in Great Britain, but it is not very easy to recognise them all.

The Noctule, or Great Bat, is the largest, measuring about four inches long and nearly fifteen inches across the wings. It flies higher than most bats, and you may be lucky enough to see it in spring and summer, when it comes out to hunt just before sunset.

. . . .

The Long-eared Bat has ears nearly as long as its body, and folds these up neatly under its wings before going to sleep.

All our Bats live on insects which they catch in the air, and also spend most of the winter fast asleep.

Fox

Foxes are found in almost all parts of the British countryside, but it requires both care and luck to see them, for Foxes often spend the day asleep under cover, and much of their hunting is done at night. Sometimes they catch rabbits, but often have to be content with smaller animals such as field mice. Although Foxes are members of the dog family, as you can see from their teeth, they are also fond of fruit and nuts, and in the autumn eat blackberries.

The parent Foxes dig a hole in the ground, called an earth, or take over an existing hole, and here the cubs are born in the spring. Cubs start coming out of their holes to play when they are about a month old, but do not leave their mothers until the autumn.

Badger

The Badger is an expert at keeping out of sight, and a family will often live in a little wood without anybody knowing it is there. The Badger is a rather heavily built animal, with broad body and short legs, and is very powerful.

In very cold climates Badgers sleep right through the winter, but in the British Isles they usually go to sleep only for a week or two at a time. Badgers make big burrows, called sets, deep in the ground, and these often have many entrance holes.

Badgers eat almost anything, sometimes catching rabbits, mice, and young birds, but for much of the time they are busy hunting for fruits, slugs, wasps' nests, and grubs of all kinds.

Otter

The Otter is one of those animals which we can recognise at a glance, but hides away so carefully that we seldom see it.

Always living near the water, the Otter is a wonderful swimmer. Its feet are webbed, but under water only the front feet are used for swimming. The Otter lives mostly on fish and is especially fond of eels, but it also eats shellfish, and if very hungry will catch birds and frogs.

Otters usually hunt at night and rest in their holes during the day. Here the young are born in the early spring. They open their eyes when about five weeks old, and soon afterwards the mother Otter teaches the young ones to swim.

Otters are active all the year round.

Grey and Common Seals

Although Seals sometimes swim up rivers, they are really sea animals, and the two kinds that live around our coasts are illustrated.

The Grey Seal (top of picture) spends most of its life out at sea, and comes to rocky parts of the coast during the breeding season in the autumn. The pups are born with thick white fur, but soon lose this. They are fed for about three weeks only before going into the water.

. . . .

The smaller Common Seal (pictured as a pair) prefers sandy beaches and flat rocks. The pups of this Seal are born about June, and they can swim almost at once.

. . . .

Seals move about rather clumsily on land, but are wonderful swimmers and can catch fish easily. Both kinds are generally rather grey in colour.

Pine Marten

The Pine Marten is one of the rarest of British animals   A few live in Scotland and in the Lake District, and perhaps also in Wales.   Many years ago the Pine Marten was quite common, and now it is coming back again to the big pine forests which are being planted.

Rather like a ferret, but much darker in colour, the Pine Marten is about eighteen inches long with a tail of twelve inches. Like most other members of the weasel family, it is a fierce hunter, and lives in the trees, jumping and running along even the thinnest branches.

Sometimes Pine Martens make their homes amongst rocks, but they usually take over an old bird's-nest or a squirrel's drey to live in.

Weasel and Stoat

The Stoat and the Weasel are much alike except in size. The Stoat is about ten inches long with a four-inch tail, while the Weasel is only eight inches long with a three-inch tail. In cold countries the Stoat's fur often turns pure white in the winter and then it is called ermine, but the tip of the tail always stays black. The Weasel does not have a black tip to its tail.

Both these little creatures are keen hunters and they are so slender that they can chase field mice and voles in their runs. Although both the Stoat and Weasel sometimes kill rabbits and birds, they live mostly on mice and so must be regarded as good friends of the farmer.

These fearless little hunters are cousins of the ferret and the otter.

Wild Cat

Except for its short tail, the Wild Cat looks like a big Tabby Cat, but it is the most savage of British animals, and nobody has ever been able to keep one as a proper pet. Apart from gamekeepers few people have ever seen one, because the Wild Cat hides away in rocky holes in the Scottish moors and forests.

When hunting for its food, the Wild Cat catches all kinds of birds as well as hares and rabbits. Sometimes it will take very young deer, and if really hungry, will not hesitate to steal a lamb.

The kittens are generally born about May, and there are usually three or four in a litter. From the moment their eyes open they are just as wild and savage as their parents.

Brown Hare and Rabbit

Although these animals look rather alike, they are different in size and habit.

The Brown Hare is very much bigger than the Rabbit, and the ears and hind legs are always much longer. The Hare's young, called leverets, are born on the ground, being well covered with fur, and their eyes open at once.

In the Scottish hills lives a different kind of Hare: it is much smaller, and its fur turns white in winter.

. . . .

The Rabbit lives in a burrow underground, and the doe digs a special burrow in which to have her young. They are quite naked and cannot see at birth. When the doe leaves them to find grass and other plants to eat, she blocks up the entrance to the burrow so carefully that it is hard to find.

Dormouse and Field Mouse

With its warm brown coat and furry tail, the Dormouse is one of the prettiest of all our wild creatures. Its name means ' sleeping mouse,' and it does indeed spend most of the winter fast asleep, snugly hidden away in a warm nest of leaves.

The Dormouse is found mostly in woods in the South of England, where there are plenty of hazel bushes ; but it seems to be getting very scarce now.

. . . .

The Field Mouse is not always a good name for this little creature, for it lives more in woods and hedges than in fields. It is about the same size as a house mouse, but the back is always a warm brown colour and its underneath is white.

The Field Mouse feeds on seeds and fruits of all kinds, as well as eating insects, and makes its home under cover.

Water Vole
and Water Shrew

Here are two animals which spend most of their time in the water.

The Water Vole has the same rather blunt nose as other voles, but is about the size of a brown rat. It feeds mostly on thick grasses and sedge stems, and you can often see one sitting by the side of a stream, chewing hard at a stem held firmly in its front feet. If you disturb it, however, the Vole jumps into the water with a loud 'plop.'

. . . .

The tiny Water Shrew has a waterproof coat like the Water Vole, but swims more like a little fish. It eats all sorts of small insects and other creatures which are found among the water weeds, and is especially fond of living in watercress beds.

Harvest Mouse
and Field Vole

The Harvest Mouse almost ties with the Shrew for being our smallest furry animal, but it belongs to the mouse family. Its real home is in the cornfields, where it builds a little round nest of grasses among the cornstalks, and with its thin little tail takes hold of the stalks to steady itself when they bend in the wind.

Unfortunately the Harvest Mouse is becoming very rare, and is found only in a few parts of Great Britain to-day.

. . . .

The Field Vole has a rather blunt nose and a rough dark coat. Its tail is very short, so you are not likely to confuse it with the long-tailed Field Mouse.

The Field Voles tunnel through the tangled grasses, but do not make real holes in the ground, and are often so plentiful that they damage the farmers' crops.

Brown Rat

The Brown Rat's real home is in Asia, but it is such a cunning animal that it has now managed to spread over almost all the world.

We find Brown Rats in the towns, but they are just as common in the countryside, and farmers regard them as their enemies. Rats eat a lot of corn and steal eggs if they get the chance, or even kill small chickens. They are the only wild animals of which we cannot say anything good and are called vermin.

The male Rat is called a buck and his mate a doe. The body of a fully grown Brown Rat is about eight inches long, with a bare tail which is always a little shorter than its body.

Red Squirrel

The Red Squirrel is smaller than the Grey Squirrel and most people think it is prettier. Although its coat changes from winter to summer, the Red Squirrel is always red-brown with white under-parts, but the ear tufts illustrated appear only in winter. Like all squirrels it is a day animal, sleeping all night in its drey.

Red Squirrels prefer pine woods, and unfortunately sometimes do damage by biting the shoots of young trees. They eat all sorts of seeds and fruits, holding the food neatly in their forepaws.

The young are born in March or April, and there may be a second family later in the year. When they are very small the mother Squirrel carries them one by one in her mouth. Sometimes she builds an extra home to move into if danger threatens.

Grey Squirrel

Although it is now very common in many parts, the Grey Squirrel does not originate in the British Isles, but was brought over here from North America.

The Grey Squirrel looks very pretty as it scampers around, and the young are particularly attractive, but it can do a lot of damage and is often described as a pest. This squirrel is very much at home in parks, because it likes living in trees such as oaks and chestnuts, biting off leafy twigs to make nests near the top of fairly tall trees. These nests are called dreys.

The Grey Squirrel may stay in its nest asleep for a few days if the weather is very cold, but it does not go to sleep for the whole winter.

Red Deer

The Red Deer is our biggest wild animal. Many years ago it lived all over the countryside, but now we find it only in big forests or on open moors such as Dartmoor and Exmoor, and in Scotland.

The male Red Deer is called a stag and the female a hind, whilst the young are known as fawns. The stag casts his antlers during spring and spends the summer growing a new pair. While they are growing, the antlers have a soft velvet skin and are easily damaged, but by September they are full size.

This is the time for roaring and battle, when a stag fights to defend his herd against a rival. But little damage is usually done, for as soon as one stag begins to lose he runs away.

Fallow Deer

Fallow Deer are the kind which we often see in parks, living in herds of twenty or more. The colour of some of their coats is very light and others very dark brown, and it is the latter kind which live wild in places such as the New Forest and Epping Forest.

The males, called bucks, grow and shed their antlers every year, and these grow bigger each year until the bucks are six or seven years old, and afterwards gradually get smaller again. The ends of the antlers are always rather flat, something like the palm of a hand with short fingers.

Fallow Deer feed mostly on grass and weeds, but they also enjoy nibbling the leaves and shoots of trees.

Their true home is in south-east Europe and Asia Minor, and the Fallow Deer were probably introduced into Britain by the Romans.

Roe Deer

The Roe Deer is one of the smallest members of the deer family and is rather like a goat in size. As in all other deer, excepting reindeer, only the buck has antlers, and he loses these every year and grows a new pair. No other deer in the world has antlers like the Roe Deer, which are rough and grow very differently as you will see in the illustration.

The buck and doe live together for most of the year, but in spring the doe goes off by herself while her fawn is born, which within a few hours can follow her around. About a fortnight later the buck joins them again.

Roe Deer are very clever at hiding away, and live in woods and forests without anybody knowing they are there. Silence and patience are needed in order to see them.

Grass Snake

The Grass Snake is our commonest and biggest snake, which sometimes grows to over four feet long. It is fond of wet places and is a fine swimmer.

Like all our other reptiles, the snakes and the lizards, the Grass Snake spends the winter in hibernation. It wakes up again in the spring, but does not lay its eggs until about July. The young are only about seven inches long, and are just like their parents in colour and pattern.

Most Grass Snakes live on frogs, but they also catch newts and toads, and will even catch small fish.

Grass Snakes make good pets ; at first they are wild, but soon settle down and can be handled safely.

Viper and Common Lizard

The Viper or Adder is our only poisonous snake. It can be recognised easily by its rather fat shape and the dark zig-zag line down its back, and may be almost any colour from brown and grey to brick-red. The Viper is seldom as much as two feet long.

They are found in England, Scotland and Wales, and like dry places on heaths and moors. They feed mostly on small animals such as mice.

. . . .

The Common Lizard is found nearly everywhere in Great Britain and Ireland. It is very active and runs quickly when disturbed. This Lizard feeds on insects and spiders, and even worms, which it catches and then crushes in its jaws.

Like the Viper, the Common Lizard does not lay eggs, but from six to twelve young are born in a family at one time.

Smooth and Crested Newts

Newts are called amphibians because they spend the first part of their lives as water creatures. When Newts grow up they develop lungs and breathe air. The Newts' eggs are laid in water in spring-time, each egg being wrapped separately in a tiny water plant leaf. During the summer the Newts usually leave the water to live on land.

Of the three different kinds of Newts found in Great Britain the two we usually see are illustrated. The pair of Smooth Newts, which are generally about four inches long, appear at the top and bottom of the picture; the other pair being the Crested or Warty Newts, which are larger and brighter in colour. In both kinds, however, the male is brighter in colour than the female, and the crests are worn only in springtime.

Slow-Worm,
Toad and Frog

Frogs and Toads belong to the same family, but are easy to distinguish, because Frogs have shiny, slippery skins, whilst those of the Toads are dry and warty.

After sleeping all the winter, these amphibious creatures wake up in the spring and find a pond or stream in which to lay their eggs—called spawn. The Frogs' eggs are laid in big masses and the Toads' in long chains. The tadpoles live in the water, feeding on minute animal life, but after the breeding season both Frogs and Toads stay mostly on land.

. . . .

The Slow-Worm is really a Lizard without legs, and generally manages to keep out of sight. Although it does not like the sun the Slow-Worm feeds in the daytime, catching and eating insects, worms, and especially slugs.

. . . .

All these creatures do good and we should always be careful never to harm them.

Series 536